W9-CTR-922

Contents

Meeting Special Needs of Children

AIMS OF THE PROGRAM

In any class, one or more students may be unable to play and perform basic motor skills effectively. If these students can't play, run, jump, and throw at an early age, they may be slow to develop essential motor skills as well as other basic learnings and social skills—or not develop them at all.

Play is a child's way of learning and integrating skills that will be used throughout life. Through play, children come to understand the world about them. Through play, children learn to move and move to learn. And as children gain play and motor skills, their feelings of self-worth and their positive self-images grow.

Most children learn to play and move through the activities of childhood. They learn by interacting with the environment and with their brothers and sisters and their peers. Handicapped children and other children with special needs often lack the opportunities to play with their peers. These children do not develop play and motor skills on their own. They need a structured, sequential curriculum to interact with their peers, gain feelings of self-worth, and achieve success—and the sooner these children can begin such a program, the better.

This Play and Motor Skills Activities Series presents a program of effective instruction strategies through which all children can achieve success in the general physical education program. It is not a pull-out program (that is, the child is not pulled out for therapy or special tutorial assistance); it is not a fix-it program (that is, the child is not segregated until all deficits are remediated). It is a positive program for each child to succeed in a play-and-motor-skills activity program. It is designed to help you, the teacher, set up sequential curricula, plan each child's instructional program, and teach effectively so that each child progresses toward desired learning outcomes.

Three Major Aims of the Program

1. To enable each child to perform basic play and motor skills at the level of his or her abilities;

2. To help each child use these skills in play and daily living activities to maximize his or her health, growth, and development, as well as joy in movement; and

3. To enhance each child's feelings of self-worth and self-confidence as a learner while moving to learn and learning to move.

BOOKS IN THE SERIES

There are eight books in this Play and Motor Skills Activities Series for preprimary through early primary grades, ages 3–7 years.

1. Locomotor Activities
2. Ball-Handling Activities
3. Stunts and Tumbling Activities
4. Health and Fitness Activities
5. Rhythmic Activities
6. Body Management Activities
7. Play Activities
8. Planning for Teaching

The seven activities books are designed to help teachers of children with handicaps and other special-needs children. Each book provides sequential curricula by skill levels. Each book is complete within its cover: sequential skills and teaching activities, games, action words, and checklists for the class's record of progress in each skill and an Individual Record of Progress (IRP) report.

Book 8, *Planning for Teaching,* is an essential companion to each of the seven activities books because it presents not only the steps for planning a teaching unit and providing for individual differences in each lesson, but it also includes a guide to incorporating social skills into units and lessons and also outlines a Home Activities Program. These two guides are particularly important for children with special needs. Because they often have limited opportunities to interact with their peers, these children need planned, sequential learning experiences to develop socially acceptable behaviors. And because special-needs children also often need extensive practice to retain a skill and generalize its use, a Home Activities Program, planned jointly by parents and teacher, can give them the necessary additional structured learning opportunities.

SEQUENTIAL CURRICULA: SUCCESS BY LEVELS

Each child and the teacher evaluate success. Success is built into the sequential curricula by levels of skills and teaching activities.

Each skill is divided into three levels: rudimentary Skill Level 1 and more refined Skill Levels 2 and 3. Each level is stated in observable behavioral movement terms. The skill levels become performance objectives. Children enter the sequential program at their own performance levels. As they add one small success to another and gain a new skill component or move to a higher skill level, they learn to listen, follow directions, practice, create, and play with others.

Within each skill level, your activities are sequenced, so the child can gain understanding progressively. Within each skill, you provide cues to meet each child's level of understanding and ability. The continuum of teaching cues is

1. verbal cues (action words) with physical assistance or prompts throughout the movement,

2. verbal cues and demonstrations,

3. verbal challenges and problem-solving cues such as "can you?" and

4. introduction of self-initiated learning activities.

GAMES

Game activities are identified for each performance objective by skill level in the seven activity books. At the end of each activity book is an alphabetized description of the games. This list includes the name of each game, formation, directions, equipment, skills involved in playing, and the type of play. Just before the list, you'll find selection criteria and ways to adapt games to different skill levels. Many of the game activities can be used to teach several objectives.

ACTION WORDS

Words for actions (step, look, catch, kick), objects (foot, ball, hand), and concepts (slow, fast, far) are used as verbal cues in teaching. These action words should be matched to the child's level of understanding. They provide a bridge to connect skill activities with other classroom learnings. In the seven activity books, action words are identified for each performance objective by skill level, and an alphabetized list of Action Words is provided at the beginning of each book. As you use this program, add words that are used in other classroom activities and delete those that the children are not ready to understand.

CHECKLISTS: A CHILD'S RECORD OF PROGRESS

In each activity book, you'll also find Individual and Class Records of Progress listing each performance objective. You can use one or both to record the entry performance level and progress of each child. The child's Individual Record of Progress can be used as part of the Individualized Educational Program (IEP). The teacher can record the child's entry performance level and progress on the child's IEP report form or use the end-of-the-year checklist report.

By observing each child performing the skills in class (e.g., during play, during teaching of the skill or in set-aside time), you can meet the special needs of each child. By using the checklists to record each child's entry level performance of objectives to be taught, you can develop an instructional plan for and evaluate the progress of each child.

Assign each child a learning task (skill component or skill level) based on lesson objectives, and plan lesson activities based on the entry performance level to help the child achieve success. Then use the checklists to record, evaluate, and report each child's progress to the parents. With this record of progress, you can review the teaching-learning activities and can make changes to improve them as necessary.

TEACHING STRATEGY

Direct Instruction

Direct Instruction is coaching on specific tasks at a skill level that allows each child to succeed. A structured and sequential curriculum of essential skills is the primary component of Direct Instruction. As the child progresses in learning, the teacher poses verbal challenges and problem-solving questions such as "can you?" and "show me!" Direct Instruction is based on the premise that success builds success and failure breeds failure.

Adaptive Instruction

Adaptive Instruction is modifying what is taught and how it is taught in order to respond to each child's special needs. Adaptive Instruction helps teachers become more responsive to individual needs. Teaching is based on the child's abilities, on what is to be taught in the lesson, and on what the child is to achieve at the end of instruction. Lesson plans are based on the child's entry performance level on the skills to be taught. Students are monitored during instruction, and the activities are adjusted to each student's needs. Positive reinforcement is provided, and ways to correct the performance or behavior are immediately demonstrated.

Children enter the curriculum at different skill levels, and they learn at different rates. The sequential curriculum helps teachers to individualize the instruction for each child in the class. Thus, the same skill can be taught in a class that includes Betty, who enters at Skill Level 1, and James, who enters at Skill Level 3, because the activities are prescribed for the class or group, but the lesson is planned in order to focus on each child's learning task, and each child is working to achieve his or her own learning task. What is important is that each child master the essential skills at a level of performance that matches his or her abilities, interests, and joy.

Since children learn skills at different rates, you might want to use the following time estimates to allot instructional time for a child to make meaningful progress toward the desired level of performance. One or two skill components can usually be mastered in the instructional time available.

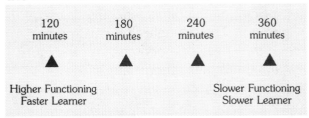

Rhythmic Skills and Activities

INTRODUCTION

Goals for Each Child

1. To demonstrate ability to perform basic rhythmic skills taught in the instructional program;

2. To use rhythmic skills in daily living activities in order to maximize healthy development and joy in movement; and

3. To gain greater feelings of self-worth and self-confidence and to gain greater ability in moving to learn and learning to move.

Rhythmic skills are an important part of every young child's movement program. Children have a natural love for music and for moving in expressive ways. Through creative movement, young children gain a better understanding of themselves and explore different ways to move.

Children begin developing rhythmic abilities during infancy as they coo in response to lullabies. As children grow, they continue to develop their abilities to respond rhythmically during early childhood and elementary grades. All young children can participate in rhythmic activities. They mime peers or their teachers. As children grow older and gain confidence in their movements and familiarity with various beats, they become more creative.

Rhythmic movement offers opportunities for incidental and direct teaching of body alignment. The younger that children are when they develop good posture, the more natural it will be as they mature.

Rhythm in movement means moving in time to a beat. Teaching children the elements of rhythm through a variety of locomotor and nonlocomotor activities (stamping, clapping, swaying) is a natural way to introduce and reinforce a child's sense of rhythm.

The elements of rhythm include:

1. Tempo: The speed of the music.

2. Beat: The basic unit of rhythm; beat can be even or uneven.

3. Meter: The way in which beats are put together to form a measure of music— 2/4, 3/4, 4/4.

4. Accent: Beats that are emphasized, usually just the first one of every measure.

5. Intensity: Loudness or softness of the music.

Children with special needs in preschool through early elementary years require planned, structured, and sequenced motor and play activities to develop rhythmic skills equal to their potentials. This book presents three levels of activities for each rhythmic skill in the following order:

1. Move to an even beat

2. Move to uneven beat

3. Accent

4. Expressive movement

5. Singing games

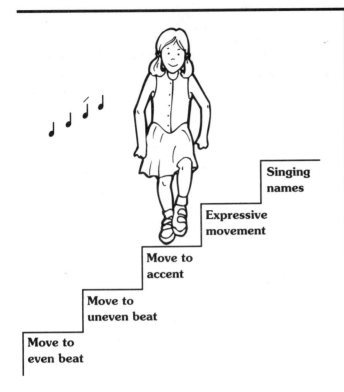

ACTION	OBJECT	CONCEPT
Bake	Ball	Afraid
Blink	Bed	Angry
Bumped	Cake	Away
Catch	Clock	Back
Clap	Crocodile	Beat
Clasp	Cup	Do this
Close	Drum	Down
Come back	Finger	Even
Crawl	Foot	Fast
Drink	Frog	Forth
Fell	Hand	Happy
Fly away	Hill	Hard
Gallop	House	Look
Go	Man	Loud
Hop	Monkey	No
Jumping	Partner	Numbers (1–6)
Knead	Piano	Of
March	Picture of different objects	Off
Move		Open
Phoned	Picture of feelings	Pretend
Play		Ready
Pour	Picture of recreation activity	Sad
Put		Show me
Roll	Pinkie	Shut
Run	Pocket	Slow
Saw	Pointer	Soft
Shout	Pot	Tall
Singing	Rabbit	Time
Skip	Records	Up
Sit	Ring	Wide
Slide	Ring man	Yes
Stamp	Spider	
Step	Spout	
Stood	Stick	
Tap	Sun	
Throw	Tall man	
Walk	Tapes	
Wash	Thumbkin	
Watch	Thump	
Wink	Water spout	

GETTING STARTED

To begin, decide which rhythmic skills you will teach. You can plan a unit or a week or a day or a year. You may decide to teach all skills in this book. Or you may select just a few. Review the checklist for each skill objective you select to teach. Become familiar with the skill components. Next, decide which action words and games you will use in teaching these skills.

Action Words

The words you use are teaching cues. Select ones your children will understand. For each of the rhythmic skills, action words are listed by skill level, and an alphabetized list of words for all the skills in this book is provided below. Circle the words you will use in teaching. If the words you selected prove too difficult for your students, cross them out. Add others that are more appropriate for your children. Star those words that work well.

Games and Play Activities

For each skill level, you'll find a list of games; select the activity matched to the skills you plan to teach. At the end of this book, you'll find a list of games along with a description of each of them. You'll note that some of the games can be used to teach more than one skill. Use this master list to note those games and play activities that work well and those that do not. Make your comments right on the game listed, or set up a similar format for the games you have selected and make your comments on that sheet. This kind of information can help you plan successful teaching activities.

Equipment

One or more of the following pieces of equipment will be needed for most of the rhythmic skill and game activities:

1. Drum or sticks for keeping beat.
2. Piano or records for keeping beat.
3. Pictures of feelings of common daily living and play events, activities, and ideas.

Space

Rhythmic activities require enough space for each child to move comfortably and safely. The size of the space depends on the equipment available for the activities and games selected and on the number of children in the class. A multipurpose room and a playground are desirable.

Health and Safety

Space and the equipment should be arranged for safety (provide mats for possible falls). Children with special visual needs may need a tour of the space and equipment before the lesson. A buddy can be assigned to be near the child when the lesson is taught. Children with special hearing needs may need to be placed on the hardwood floor to better hear and feel the music vibrations. The teacher should be positioned to observe all the children during the lesson activities.

Organization: Learning Centers

Learning centers are one of the best types of class organization. You can plan small group learning centers when you know each child's level of performance of the rhythmic skill to be taught. Learning centers can be used to group children by levels of ability or to mix children of different levels of ability. The number of learning centers and their purpose will depend on the number of teachers and support personnel: aides, parent volunteers, older peer models.

To set up a learning center, you should consider the following:

1. Purpose	Skills to be taught and practiced
2. Levels	Levels 1, 2, and 3, or only one, determined by size of class, space, equipment, support personnel
3. Grouping	Same or mixed skill levels
4. Physical setting	Location, such as playground or multipurpose room; equipment available; existing physical boundaries, such as walls, or space to make boundaries with chairs, benches, mats, tapes
5. Activities	Type of game or instructional activity such as moving to even, uneven, or accented beats, expressive communication, and singing games

LEARNING CENTERS: RHYTHMIC ACTIVITIES

LEARNING CENTER 1

Location: playground

Skill: expressive movement

Activity: imitate different animals or objects; greetings: hello, goodbye; feeling: happy, sad

Grouping: Children at same or different skill levels

LEARNING CENTER 2

Location: classroom

Skill: move to even beat, uneven beat, accented beat

Activity: locomotor activities, tapping sticks, beating drum

Grouping: Children at same or different skill levels

RECORDS FOR RHYTHMIC ACTIVITIES

1. **Creative Movement and Rhythmic Exploration**
   Hap Palmer (AR 533)

2. **Easy Does It—Activity Songs for Basic Motor Skill Development**
   Hap Palmer (AR 581)

3. **Feel of Music**
   Hap Palmer (AR 556)

4. **Getting to Know Myself**
   Hap Palmer (AR 543)

5. **Homemade Bond**
   Hap Palmer (AR 546)

6. **Ideas, Thoughts, Feelings**
   Hap Palmer (AR 549)

7. **Learning Basic Skills Through Music, I and II**
   Hap Palmer (AR 514 and AR 522)

8. **Modern Tunes for Rhythms and Instruments**
   Hap Palmer (AR 523)

9. **Movin'**
   Hap Palmer (AR 546)

Educational Activities
P.O. Box 392
Freeport, NY 11520

or

Children's Music Center
5373 West Pico Blvd.
Los Angeles, CA 90019

---

1. **Little Favorites**
   (B 116)

2. **Songs for Children with Special Needs**
   Francis Cole (1, 2, and 3)

Bowmar Records/Noble Pub.
P.O. Box 25308
1901 N. Walnut St.
Oklahoma City, Ok 73125

Lively Music for Lummi Sticks
(KIM 2000)

Kimbo Educational Records
P.O. Box 477F
Long Branch, NJ 07740

Early Early Childhood Songs
Ella Jenkins (FC 7630)

Folkway Records
Birchtree Group
180 Alexander St.
Princeton, NJ 08540

Rhythm Makers
Ruth White

Tom Thumb Records
Rhythm Productions
Whitney Blvd., Box 34485
Los Angeles, CA 90035

Rhythmic Activities

MOVE TO AN EVEN BEAT: SKILL LEVEL 1

Performance Objective

The child with ability to clap or move (stamp, step, tap), given 16 even drumbeats at varying tempos, can demonstrate the following skill components three consecutive times:

Within a clear space of 20 feet, the child can

1. clap or move (stamp, step, tap, or move trunk) to eight consecutive beats at moderate tempo, and

2. clap or move (stamp, step, tap, or move trunk) to eight consecutive beats at fast tempo.

Action Words

Actions: Clap, go, hop, run, stamp, step, tap, walk

Objects: Drum, finger, foot, hand, piano, records, stick, tapes

Concepts: Do this, even, fast, look, numbers (1–6), ready, show me, slow

Games

- Baa, Baa, Black Sheep
- Brother John
- Count to Six Fast
- Diddle Diddle Dumpling
- Even-Uneven Tempo Relay
- The Farmer in the Dell
- Follow the Drum
- Hit the Beat
- Mary Had a Little Lamb
- Mulberry Bush
- Ten Little Indians
- Twinkle, Twinkle, Little Star
- Yankee Doodle

TEACHING ACTIVITIES

If a child requires assistance to respond,

1. give verbal cues and physical assistance.
Face the child, grasp his or her wrists, and guide hands through clapping motion; assist the child for eight consecutive beats. Give the child specific verbal instructions throughout (in sign language, bliss symbols, action cues), such as "Do this."

clap hands clap hands (4/4 time)

clap clap clap hands (repeat)

2. give verbal cues with demonstration.
Use a model or have the child watch you clap hands together to an even beat eight times, moving hips, head, or shoulders. Then have the child perform the action. Use specific verbal instructions (as in 1 above with the modeling).

If a child can respond without assistance,

3. give a verbal challenge in the form of a problem: "Who can do this?"
a. Clap your hands to this beat:

1 2 3 4   1 2 3 4

b. Stamp your feet to this beat:

♩ ♩ ♩ ♩ | ♩ ♩ ♩ ♩
1 2 3 4   1 2 3 4

c. Move body while sitting. Tap finger. Tap foot.

d. Sing "Mulberry Bush" and clap your hands to the beat.

e. Sing "Baa, Baa, Black Sheep" and tap your feet to the beat.

f. Variations: Use records, tapes, or beating a drum with songs.

4. introduce self-initiated learning activities.
Set up the equipment (record, tape recorder) and space for moving to an even beat. Provide time at the beginning of the lesson and free time for independent learning after the child understands the skills to be used. You may ask the child to create a game activity to play alone or with others (partner or small group), using the record or tapes.

5. Variations: Play a game, such as Mulberry Bush or Follow the Drum, that incorporates moving to an even beat.

Performance Objective

The child with acquisition of Skill Level 1 and the ability to move (walk, run, hop), given 16 even drumbeats at varying tempos, can demonstrate the following skill components three consecutive times:

Within a clear space of 20 feet, the child can

3. move (walk, run, hop) to eight consecutive beats at moderate tempo, and

4. move (walk, run, hop) to eight consecutive beats at fast tempo.

Skills to Review

1. Clap or move (stamp, step, tap, or move trunk) to eight consecutive beats at moderate tempo, and

2. clap or move (stamp, step, tap, or move trunk) to eight consecutive beats at fast tempo.

Action Words

Actions: Clap, go, hop, run, stamp, step, tap, walk

Objects: Drum, finger, foot, hand, piano, records, stick, tapes

Concepts: Do this, even, fast, look, numbers (1–6), ready, show me, slow

Games

- Baa, Baa, Black Sheep
- Brother John
- Count to Six Fast
- Diddle Diddle Dumpling
- Even-Uneven Tempo Relay
- The Farmer in the Dell
- Follow the Drum
- Hit the Beat
- Mary Had a Little Lamb
- Mulberry Bush
- Ten Little Indians
- Twinkle, Twinkle, Little Star
- Yankee Doodle

TEACHING ACTIVITIES

If a child requires assistance to respond,

1. give verbal cues and physical assistance.
Face the child, grasp his or her hand, and initiate walking (running, hopping) to an even beat. Assist child for eight beats, then let child continue moving for eight or more beats. Give the child specific verbal instructions throughout (in sign language, bliss symbols, action cues), such as "Do this."

one, two, three, four, five, six, ready, go:

walk, walk, walk, walk (repeat)

2. give verbal cues with demonstration.
Use a model or have the child watch you clap hands together to an even beat at moderate speed eight times, after eight introductory beats. Then have the child perform the action. Use specific verbal instructions (as in 1 above with the modeling). Then change tempo from moderate to fast.

If a child can respond without assistance,

3. give a verbal challenge in the form of a problem: "Who can do this?"

a. Walk to the beat of the drum. Change tempo from moderate to fast.

one, two, three, four, five, six, ready, go:

walk, walk, walk, walk (repeat)

b. Hop to the record's beat.

c. Run to the beat as my hands clap together.

d. Walk to the beat of "Mary Had a Little Lamb."

e. Variation: Use records, tapes, or beat a drum with songs.

4. introduce self-initiated learning activities.
Set up the equipment (record, tape recorder) and space for moving to an even beat. Provide time at the beginning of the lesson and free time for independent learning after the child understands the skills to be used. You may ask the child to create a game activity to play alone or with others (partner or small group), using the record or tapes.

5. Variations: Play a game, such as Mulberry Bush or Follow the Drum, that incorporates moving to an even beat.

MOVE TO AN EVEN BEAT: SKILL LEVEL 3

Performance Objective

The child with acquisition of Skill Level 2 or a level of performance appropriate for the child's level of functioning can clap or move to an even beat at varying tempos, and maintain that level over six weeks.

Given activities that require the skill, the child can

1. play two or more games listed below at home or school, and
2. play with equipment selected by teacher and parent(s).

Skills to Review

1. Level 1 even beat. Clap or move (stamp, step, tap, or move trunk) to eight consecutive beats at moderate tempo, and
2. clap or move (stamp, step, tap, or move trunk) to eight consecutive beats at fast tempo.
3. Level 2 even beat. Move (walk, run, hop) to eight consecutive beats at moderate tempo, and
4. move (walk, run, hop) to eight consecutive beats at fast tempo.

Action Words

Actions: Clap, go, hop, run, stamp, step, tap, walk

Objects: Drum, finger, foot, hand, piano, records, stick, tapes

Concepts: Do this, even, fast, look, numbers (1–6), ready, show me, slow

Games

- Baa, Baa, Black Sheep
- Brother John
- Count to Six Fast
- Diddle Diddle Dumpling
- Even-Uneven Tempo Relay
- The Farmer in the Dell
- Follow the Drum
- Hit the Beat
- Mary Had a Little Lamb
- Mulberry Bush
- Ten Little Indians
- Twinkle, Twinkle, Little Star
- Yankee Doodle

TEACHING ACTIVITIES FOR MAINTENANCE

In Teaching

1. Provide the child with teaching cues (verbal and nonverbal, such as demonstration, modeling, imitating) for moving to an even beat that involve the skill components the child has achieved in compatible teaching and play activities. Bring to the child's attention the skill components he or she has already achieved. Provide positive reinforcement and feedback for the child.

2. Use games that require moving to an even beat and that involve imitating, modeling, and demonstrating.

3. Observe and assess each child's maintenance at the end of two weeks. Repeat at the end of four weeks (if maintained) and six weeks after initial date of attainment.

▲ Box in the skill level to be maintained on the child's Class Record of Progress. Note the date the child attained target level of performance (defined by teacher alone or co-planned with parents).

▲ Two weeks after attainment, observe the child. Is the level maintained? If child does not demonstrate the skill components at the desired level of performance, indicate the skill components that need reteaching or reinforcing in the comments sheet on the Class Record of Progress. Reschedule teaching time, and co-plan with parents the home activities necessary to reinforce child's achievement of the skill components and maintenance of attainment.

▲ Continue to observe the child, and reteach and reinforce until the child maintains that level of performance for six weeks.

▲ Plan teaching activities incorporating these components so that the child can continually use and reinforce them and can acquire new ones over the year.

▲ When the child can understand it, make a checklist poster illustrating the child's achievements. Bring the child's attention to these skill components in various compatible play and game activities throughout the year. Have the child help others—a partner or a small group.

In Co-Planning with Parent(s)

1. Encourage the parent(s) to reinforce the child's achievement of the skill components in everyday play and living activities in the home.

▲ Provide key action words for the parent(s) to emphasize.

▲ Give the parent(s) a list of play and games to use in playing with the child, thus reinforcing the skill components the child has achieved and needs support to maintain.

▲ Give the parent(s) a list of rhythmic activities that can be done at home with the child, such as
   a. Moving (walking, running, hopping) to the beat of "Follow the Drum."
   b. Hopping to the even beat of "Mulberry Bush."
   c. Walking to the even beat of music on your stereo set at home.
   d. Clapping to the even beat of the music on *Sesame Street*.
   e. Moving to the beat of the music for the birthday party game, Musical Chairs.

2. Set up a time every two weeks to interact with the parent(s) and exchange feedback on the child's progress.

Performance Objective

The child with ability to clap or move (stamp, step, tap), given four measures of uneven rhythm at moderate tempo, can demonstrate the following skill components three consecutive times:

Within a clear space of 20 feet, the child can

1. clap hands to two consecutive measures of uneven rhythm at moderate tempo, and
2. tap or stamp feet to two consecutive measures of uneven rhythm at moderate tempo.

Action Words

Actions: Clap, gallop, go, skip, slide, stamp, tap, watch

Objects: Finger, foot, hand, piano, records, stick

Concepts: Beat, do this, numbers (1–4), ready, show me, uneven

Games

- Eensy Weensy Spider
- Even-Uneven Temp Relay
- Follow the Drum
- One, Two, Buckle My Shoe
- Ring Around the Rosy

TEACHING ACTIVITIES

If a child requires assistance to respond,

1. give verbal cues and physical assistance.
Face the child, grasp his or her wrists and guide hands through clapping motion, or grasp the child's arm and move it to the uneven beat. Give the child specific verbal instructions throughout (in sign language, bliss symbols, action cues), such as "Do this."

clap, clap, clap your hands (repeat) or do this:

tap, tap, tap your feet

2. give verbal cues with demonstration.
Use a model or have the child watch you clap hands together or move to an uneven beat at moderate tempo. Then have the child perform the action. Use specific verbal instructions (as in 1 above with the modeling).

If a child can respond without assistance,

3. **give a verbal challenge in the form of a problem: "Who can do this?"**

a. Clap your hands to this beat:

♩ ♩ ♫ ♩ | ♩ ♩ ♫ ♩

one two rea-dy go clap clap clap your hands.

b. Tap your feet to this beat:

♩ ♩ ♫ ♩ | ♩ ♩ ♫ ♩

one two rea-dy go tap tap tap your feet.

c. Sing "One, Two, Buckle My Shoe" and clap your hands to the beat.

4. **introduce self-initiated learning activities.**
Set up the equipment (record, tape recorder) and space for moving to an uneven beat. Provide time at the beginning of the lesson and free time for independent learning after the child understands the skills to be used. You may ask the child to create a game activity to play alone or with others (partner or small group), using the record or tapes.

5. **Variations:** Play a game, such as One, Two, Buckle My Shoe or Follow the Drum, that incorporates moving to an uneven beat.

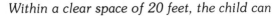

Performance Objective

The child with acquisition of Skill Level 1 and the ability to move (gallop, skip, slide), given four measures of uneven rhythm at moderate tempo, can demonstrate the following skill components three consecutive times:

Within a clear space of 20 feet, the child can

3. move (gallop, skip, slide) to two consecutive measures of uneven rhythm at moderate tempo.

Skills to Review

1. Clap hands to two consecutive measures of uneven rhythm at moderate tempo, and
2. tap or stamp feet to two consecutive measures of uneven rhythm at moderate tempo.

Action Words

Actions: Clap, gallop, go, skip, slide, stamp, tap, watch

Objects: Finger, foot, hand, piano, records, stick

Concepts: Beat, do this, numbers (1–4), ready, show me, uneven

Games

- Eensy Weensy Spider
- Even-Uneven Tempo Relay
- Follow the Drum
- One, Two, Buckle My Shoe
- Ring Around the Rosy

TEACHING ACTIVITIES

If a child requires assistance to respond,

1. give verbal cues and physical assistance.
Hold the child's hand to assist with galloping or skipping, or face child and hold both hands to assist with sliding, for two measures of uneven rhythm. Let child continue moving to two or more measures. Give the child specific verbal instructions throughout (in sign language, bliss symbols, action cues), such as "Do this."

watch me gal-lop (repeat) let's both gal-lop
or

watch me slid-ing (repeat) let's go slid-ing

2. give verbal cues with demonstration.
Use a model or have the child watch you gallop or skip forward, or slide sideways, to an uneven beat four times. Then have the child perform the action. Use specific verbal instructions (as in 1 above with the modeling).

If a child can respond without assistance,

3. give a verbal challenge in the form of a problem: "Who can do this?"

a. Gallop to the uneven beat as I clap my hands.

♪ ♩ ♪ ♩

gal-lop, gal-lop,

(repeat)

b. Slide to the uneven beat of the record "One, Two, Buckle My Shoe."

♪ ♩ ♪ ♩

slid-ing, slid-ing

(repeat)

c. Skip to the uneven beat of a song.

♪ ♩ ♪ ♩ ♪ ♩ ♪ ♩

skip-ping skip-ping skip-ping skip-ping

4. introduce self-initiated learning activities.
Set up the equipment (record, tape recorder) and space for moving to an uneven beat. Provide time at the beginning of the lesson and free time for independent learning after the child understands the skills to be used. You may ask the child to create a game activity to play alone or with others (partner or small group), using the record or tapes.

5. Variations: Play a game, such as One, Two, Buckle My Shoe or Follow the Drum, that incorporates moving to an uneven beat.

MOVE TO AN UNEVEN BEAT: SKILL LEVEL 3

Performance Objective

The child with acquisition of Skill Level 2 or a level of performance appropriate for the child's level of functioning can maintain that level over six weeks.

Given activities that require the skill, the child can

1. play two or more games listed below at home or school, and
2. play with equipment selected by teacher and parent(s).

Skills to Review

1. Level 1 uneven beat. Clap hands to two consecutive measures of uneven rhythm at moderate tempo and
2. tap feet to two consecutive measures of uneven rhythm at moderate tempo.
3. Level 2 uneven beat. Move (gallop, skip, slide) to two consecutive measures of uneven rhythm at moderate tempo.

Action Words

Actions: Clap, gallop, go, skip, slide, stamp, tap, watch

Objects: Finger, foot, hand, piano, records, stick

Concepts: Beat, do this, numbers (1–4), ready, show me, uneven

Games

- Eensy Weensy Spider
- Even-Uneven Tempo Relay
- Follow the Drum
- One, Two, Buckle My Shoe
- Ring Around the Rosy

TEACHING ACTIVITIES FOR MAINTENANCE

In Teaching

1. Provide the child with teaching cues (verbal and nonverbal, such as demonstration, modeling, imitating) for moving to an uneven beat that involve the skill components the child has achieved in compatible teaching and play activities. Bring to the child's attention the skill components he or she has already achieved. Provide positive reinforcement and feedback for the child.

2. Use games that require moving to an uneven beat and that involve imitating, modeling, and demonstrating.

3. Observe and assess each child's maintenance at the end of two weeks. Repeat at the end of four weeks (if maintained) and six weeks after initial date of attainment.

▲ Box in the skill level to be maintained on the child's Class Record of Progress. Note the date the child attained target level of performance (defined by teacher alone or co-planned with parents).

▲ Two weeks after attainment, observe the child. Is the level maintained? If child does not demonstrate the skill components at the desired level of performance, indicate the skill components that need reteaching or reinforcing in the comments sheet on the Class Record of Progress. Reschedule teaching time, and co-plan with parents the home activities necessary to reinforce child's achievement of the skill components and maintenance of attainment.

▲ Continue to observe the child, and reteach and reinforce until the child maintains that level of performance for six weeks.

▲ Plan teaching activities incorporating these components so that the child can continually use and reinforce them and can acquire new ones over the year.

▲ When the child can understand it, make a check-list poster illustrating the child's achievements. Bring the child's attention to these skill components in various compatible play and game activities throughout the year. Have the child help others—a partner or a small group.

In Co-Planning with Parent(s)

1. Encourage the parent(s) to reinforce the child's achievement of the skill components in everyday play and living activities in the home.

▲ Provide key action words for the parent(s) to emphasize.

▲ Give the parent(s) a list of play and games to use in playing with the child, thus reinforcing the skill components the child has achieved and needs support to maintain.

▲ Give the parent(s) a list of rhythmic activities that can be done at home with the child, such as

   a. Moving (galloping, sliding, skipping) to the beat of "Follow the Drum."

   b. Galloping to the uneven beat of "One, Two, Buckle My Shoe."

   c. Sliding to the uneven beat of the music on your stereo set at home.

   d. Clapping to the uneven beat of the music on *Sesame Street*.

   e. Moving to the beat of the music for the birthday party game, Musical Chairs.

2. Set up a time every two weeks to interact with the parent(s) and exchange feedback on the child's progress.

ACCENT: SKILL LEVEL 1

Performance Objective

The child with ability to clap or move (stamp, step, tap), given six measures of rhythm (four beats each with accent on first beat), can demonstrate the following skill components three consecutive times:

Within a clear space of 20 feet, the child can

1. clap or move (stamp, step, tap, or move trunk), accenting the first beat of four consecutive measures.

Action Words

Actions: Clap, move, stamp, step

Objects: Drum, foot, hand, piano, records, stick, tapes

Concepts: Beat, hard, loud, numbers (1–4), soft

Games

- Around We Go
- Baa, Baa, Black Sheep
- Brother John
- Diddle Diddle Dumpling
- Follow the Drum
- Hit the Beat
- Mary Had a Little Lamb
- Ten Little Indians
- Yankee Doodle

TEACHING ACTIVITIES

If a child requires assistance to respond,

1. give verbal cues and physical assistance.
Face the child, grasp his or her wrists and guide hands through clapping motion. Assist the child in clapping to give a stronger accent on the first of four beats for four measures after listening to two measures. Then move the child's arm, head, etc., so that the first beat is accented. Give the child specific verbal instructions throughout (in sign language, bliss symbols, action cues), such as "Listen to the beats," "Clap hard on the first beat: **1** 2 3 4 / **1** 2 3 4 / **1** 2 3 4."

2. give verbal cues with demonstration.
Use a model or have the child watch you clap, accenting the first of four beats with a loud clap or movement with the body. Then have the child perform the action. Use specific verbal instructions (as in 1 above with the modeling).

If a child can respond without assistance,

3. give a verbal challenge in the form of a problem: "Who can do this?"
a. Clap your hands to this beat, clapping louder on the first beat.

♩ ♩ ♫ ♩ | ♩ ♩ ♫ ♩

one two rea-dy go **clap** clap clap your hands.

b. Stamp your feet on the first beat that is accented.

♩ ♩ ♫ ♩ | ♩ ♩ ♫ ♩

one two rea-dy go **stamp** stamp stamp your feet.

c. Sing "Brother John" and clap loud on the first beat.
d. Variations: Use records or tapes or beat a drum with songs.

4. introduce self-initiated learning activities.
Set up the equipment (record, tape recorder) and space for moving to an accented beat. Provide time at the beginning of the lesson and free time for independent learning after the child understands the skills to be used. You may ask the child to create a game activity to play alone or with others (partner or small group), using the record or tapes.

5. Variations: Play a game, such as Hit the Beat or Follow the Drum, that incorporates moving to an accented beat.

ACCENT: SKILL LEVEL 2

Performance Objective

The child with acquisition of Skill Level 1, given six measures of rhythm (four beats with accent on first beat), can demonstrate the following skill components three consecutive times:

Within a clear space of 20 feet, the child can

2. clap or move (stamp, step, tap), accenting the second, third, or fourth beat on four consecutive measures.

Skills to Review

1. Clap or move (stamp, step, tap, or move trunk), accenting the first beat of four consecutive measures.

Action Words

Actions: Clap, move, stamp, step

Objects: Drum, foot, hand, piano, records, stick, tapes

Concepts: Beat, hard, loud, numbers (1–4), soft

Games

- Around We Go
- Baa, Baa, Black Sheep
- Brother John
- Diddle Diddle Dumpling
- Follow the Drum
- Hit the Beat
- Mary Had a Little Lamb
- Ten Little Indians
- Yankee Doodle

TEACHING ACTIVITIES

If a child requires assistance to respond,

1. give verbal cues and physical assistance.
Face the child, grasp his or her wrists, and start clapping motion to accent second, third, or fourth beat. Then move the child's arm, head, etc., so that the second or third beat is accented. Give the child specific verbal instructions throughout (in sign language, bliss symbols, action cues), such as "Listen to the loud beats," or "Move like this: little step, by step, little, little."

2. give verbal cues with demonstration.
Use a model or have the child watch you accent a beat by clapping loud or moving on the second, third, or last beat of four beats. Then have the child perform the action. Use specific verbal instructions (as in 1 above with the modeling).

If a child can respond without assistance,

3. give a verbal challenge in the form of a problem: "Who can do this?"

a. Clap your hands to this beat, clapping louder on the second beat.

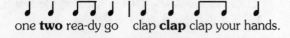
one **two** rea-dy go   clap **clap** clap your hands.

b. Stamp your feet on the accented third beat. On the accented fourth beat.

♩ ♩ ♫ ♩ | ♩ ♩ ♫ ♩ ♩

one two **rea**-dy go   stamp stamp stamp your **feet.**

c. Sing "Baa Baa Black Sheep."

d. Variations: Use records or tapes or beat a drum with songs.

4. introduce self-initiated learning activities.
Set up the equipment (record, tape recorder) and space for moving to an accented beat. Provide time at the beginning of the lesson and free time for independent learning after the child understands the skills to be used. You may ask the child to create a game activity to play alone or with others (partner or small group), using the record or tapes.

5. Variations: Play a game, such as Hit the Beat or Follow the Drum, that incorporates moving to an accented beat.

ACCENT: SKILL LEVEL 3

Performance Objective

The child with acquisition of Skill Level 2 or a level of performance appropriate for the child's level of functioning can maintain that level over six weeks.

Given activities that require the skill, the child can

1. play with two or more games listed below at home or school, and
2. play with equipment selected by teacher and parent(s).

Skills to Review

1. Level 1 accent. Clap or move (stamp, step, tap, or move trunk), accenting the first beat of four consecutive measures.
2. Level 2 accent. Clap or move (stamp, step, tap), accenting the second, third, or fourth beat of four consecutive measures.

Action Words

Actions: Clap, move, stamp, step

Objects: Drum, foot, hand, piano, records, stick, tapes

Concepts: Beat, hard, loud, numbers (1–4), soft

Games

- Around We Go
- Baa, Baa, Black Sheep
- Brother John
- Diddle Diddle Dumpling
- Follow the Drum
- Hit the Beat
- Mary Had a Little Lamb
- Ten Little Indians
- Yankee Doodle

TEACHING ACTIVITIES FOR MAINTENANCE

In Teaching

1. Provide the child with teaching cues (verbal and nonverbal, such as demonstration, modeling, imitating) for moving to an accented beat that involve the skill components the child has achieved in compatible teaching and play activities. Bring to the child's attention the skill components he or she has already achieved. Provide positive reinforcement and feedback for the child.

2. Use games that require moving to an accented beat and that involve imitating, modeling, and demonstrating.

3. Observe and assess each child's maintenance at the end of two weeks. Repeat at the end of four weeks (if maintained) and six weeks after initial date of attainment.

▲ Box in the skill level to be maintained on the child's Class Record of Progress. Note the date the child attained target level of performance (defined by teacher alone or co-planned with parents).

▲ Two weeks after attainment, observe the child. Is the level maintained? If child does not demonstrate the skill components at the desired level of performance, indicate the skill components that need reteaching or reinforcing in the comments sheet on the Class Record of Progress. Reschedule teaching time, and co-plan with parents the home activities necessary to reinforce child's achievement of the skill components and maintenance of attainment.

▲ Continue to observe the child, and reteach and reinforce until the child maintains that level of performance for six weeks.

▲ Plan teaching activities incorporating these components so that the child can continually use and reinforce them and can acquire new ones over the year.

▲ When the child can understand it, make a checklist poster illustrating the child's achievements. Bring the child's attention to these skill components in various compatible play and game activities throughout the year. Have the child help others—a partner or a small group.

In Co-Planning with Parent(s)

1. Encourage the parent(s) to reinforce the child's achievement of the skill components in everyday play and living activities in the home.

▲ Provide key action words for the parent(s) to emphasize.

▲ Give the parent(s) a list of play and games to use in playing with the child, thus reinforcing the skill components the child has achieved and needs support to maintain.

▲ Give the parent(s) a list of rhythmic activities that can be done at home with the child, such as
   a. Walking to even beat of music or record and stamping foot or clapping hands to accent first beat.
   b. Clapping to even beat of the music on *Sesame Street* (clap on first beat).

2. Set up a time every two weeks to interact with the parent(s) and exchange feedback on the child's progress.

EXPRESSIVE MOVEMENT: SKILL LEVEL 1

Performance Objective

The child with ability to move the body or body parts, given pictures or demonstrations of objects, gestures, and feelings known to the child and found in the child's environment, can demonstrate the following skill components three consecutive times (the teacher or the child selects objects, gestures, and feelings to demonstrate):

Within a clear space of 20 feet, the child can

1. move, imitating two out of three objects, such as dog greeting child at door, cat sleeping, zoo animals, airplane flying, train moving, trees or flowers or grass moving, and

2. move, imitating two out of three gestures, such as hello, goodbye, yes, no, welcome, and

3. move, expressing two out of three feelings, such as happiness, sadness, like, dislike, anger.

Action Words

(These are examples. Those words you use will depend on your selections.)

Actions: Frown, jump, jump up and down, laugh, move, nod, shake, smile, swing, walk, wave, wiggle

Objects: Animals, flowers, grass, muscle, piano, pictures, trees, vehicles

Concepts: Anger, back, down, dislike, goodbye, happy, hello, high, like, low, moving, no, pretend, sad, up, welcome, yes

Games

(These are examples. Choose games familiar to your students.)

- A Tiny Little Mouse
- Bunny Hop
- Happy Story
- If You're Happy
- Isn't It Fun?
- Jack-in-the-Box
- Mulberry Bush
- My Airplane
- Wiggle Like a Snake
- Zoo Song

TEACHING ACTIVITIES

The following activities are examples. Substitute the names of daily living or play activities selected by you or the child (when the child is ready to do so).

If a child requires assistance to respond,

1. give verbal cues and physical assistance.
Face the child, and assist him or her in moving body parts like an elephant (arms down, clasp hands, body bent over, lumbering slow steps); an airplane (arms out for wings, tilt body side to side, walk fast like flying). Say, "Move like an airplane," "Show me your wings."

Initiate movement by manipulating child's body into position to show happiness (smiling, jumping, swinging arms, skipping). Give the child specific verbal instructions throughout (in sign language, bliss symbols, action cues), such as "Do this, be sad," "Make your face sad," "Be droopy, drag your feet, pout."

Put child's body into position to show anger. Say, "Do this, be angry," "Stamp your feet, scowl, look angry."

2. give verbal cues with demonstration.
Use a model or have the child watch you demonstrate movements showing happiness (smile, jump, randomly skip about in various directions, leap). Model movements showing sadness (pout, hang head down, drag feet, shuffle). Model movements showing anger (scowl, touch face, make quick thrusting gestures, stamp, jump hard). Model movements showing fear (hide face, move cautiously, look about, sit coiled up). Then have the child perform the action. Use specific verbal instructions (as in 1 above with the modeling).

If a child can respond without assistance,

3. give a verbal challenge in the form of a problem: "Who can do this?"

a. Move like an airplane flying fast across the sky.

b. Move like an elephant in the zoo.

c. Move like your dog when he greets you at the front door.

d. Move like a choo-choo train moving across the tracks.

e. Move around the room thinking about how happy you will be on your birthday.

f. Move around the room thinking about how sad you will be if one of your friends moves far away.

g. Move around the room thinking about how angry you will be if your brother gets you in trouble for something you did not do.

h. Variations: Use music depicting different feelings, and have child move to the music. Use pictures showing feelings, and have children move to imitate pictures.

4. introduce self-initiated learning activities.
Set up the equipment (record, tape recorder) and space for expressive movement. Provide time at the beginning of the lesson and free time for independent learning after the child understands the skills to be used. You may ask the child to create a game activity to play alone or with others (partner or small group), using the record or tapes.

5. Variations: Play a game, such as Isn't It Fun? or Jack-in-the-Box, that incorporates moving to imitate objects, gestures, and express feelings.

EXPRESSIVE MOVEMENT: SKILL LEVEL 2

Performance Objective

The child with acquisition of Skill Level 1, given pictures or demonstrations of ideas or events known to the child and found in the child's environment, can demonstrate the following skill components three consecutive times (the teacher or the child selects the ideas or events):

Within a clear space of 20 feet, the child can

4. perform a series of movements, communicating two out of three daily events or activities to others, such as getting dressed, brushing teeth, combing or brushing hair, going to sleep, reading a book, welcoming a friend coming to play and

5. perform a series of movements, communicating two out of three play events or activities to others, such as playing ball, climbing a jungle gym, swinging on a swing, swimming or wading in a pool, moving to music (dancing).

Skills to Review

1. Move, imitating two out of three objects, such as dog greeting child at door, cat sleeping, zoo animals, airplane flying, train moving, trees or flowers or grass moving, and

2. move, imitating two out of three gestures, such as hello, goodbye, yes, no, welcome, and

3. move, expressing two out of three feelings, such as happiness, sadness, like, dislike, anger.

Action Words

(These are examples. The words you use will depend on your selections.)

Actions: Frown, jump, jump up and down, laugh, move, nod, shake, smile, swing, walk, wave, wiggle

Objects: Animals, flowers, grass, muscle, piano, pictures, trees, vehicles

Concepts: Anger, back, down, dislike, goodbye, happy, hello, high, like, moving, low, no, pretend, sad, up, welcome, yes

Games

(These are examples. Choose games familiar to your students.)

- A Tiny Little Mouse
- Bunny Hop
- Happy Story
- If You're Happy
- Isn't It Fun?
- Jack-in-the-Box
- Mulberry Bush
- My Airplane
- Wiggle Like a Snake
- Zoo Song

TEACHING ACTIVITIES

The following activities are examples. Substitute the names of daily living or play activities selected by you or child (when the child is ready to do so).

If a child requires assistance to respond,

1. give verbal cues and physical assistance.
Show the child pictures of the activities selected. Have child move to imitate picture. Assist child with these actions. Give the child specific verbal instructions throughout (in sign language, bliss symbols, action cues), such as "See the child playing in the sandbox?" "Show me how you play in the sandbox."

2. give verbal cues with demonstration.
Use a model or have the child watch you model the actions of the selected activities. Exaggerate and use large movements. Then have the child perform the action. Use specific verbal instructions (as in 1 above with the modeling).

If a child can respond without assistance,

3. give a verbal challenge in the form of a problem: "Who can do this?"
a. Move like you are getting dressed for school.

b. Move like you are washing your face and hands.

c. Move like you are playing on the swing set in the yard.

d. Move like you are climbing a jungle gym.

e. Move like you are playing in a sandbox.

f. Move like you are swimming in a pool.

g. Move like you are brushing your teeth.

4. introduce self-initiated learning activities.
Set up the equipment (record, tape recorder) and space for expressive movement. Provide time at the beginning of the lesson and free time for independent learning after the child understands the skills to be used. You may ask the child to create a game activity to play alone or with others (partner or small group), using the record or tapes.

5. Variations: Play a game, such as Isn't It Fun? or Jack-in-the-Box, that incorporates moving to communicate ideas or events in daily living or playing.

EXPRESSIVE MOVEMENT: SKILL LEVEL 3

Performance Objective

The child with acquisition of Skill Level 2 or a level of performance appropriate for the child's level of functioning can maintain that level over six weeks.

Given activities that require the skill, the child can

1. play two or more games listed below at home or school, and
2. play with equipment selected by teacher and parent(s).

Note: Skill components are listed because the child is dealing with different concepts at each level.

Skills to Review

1. Level 1 expressive movement. Move, imitating two out of three objects, and
2. move, imitating two out of three gestures, and
3. move, expressing two out of three feelings.
4. Level 2 expressive movement. Perform series of movements, communicating two out of three daily events or activities, and
5. perform a series of movements, communicating two out of three play events or activities.

Action Words

(These are examples. The words you use will depend on your selections.)

Actions: Frown, jump, jump up and down, laugh, move, nod, shake, smile, swing, walk, wave, wiggle

Objects: Animals, flowers, grass, muscle, piano, pictures, trees, vehicles

Concepts: Angry, back, down, dislike, good-bye, happy, hello, high, like, moving, low, no, pretend, sad, up, welcome, yes

Games

(These are examples. Choose games familiar to your students.)

- A Tiny Little Mouse
- Bunny Hop
- Happy Story
- If You're Happy
- Isn't It Fun?
- Jack-in-the-Box
- Mulberry Bush
- My Airplane
- Wiggle Like a Snake
- Zoo Song

TEACHING ACTIVITIES FOR MAINTENANCE

In Teaching

1. Provide the child with teaching cues (verbal and nonverbal, such as demonstration, modeling, imitating) for expressive movement that involve the skill components the child has achieved in compatible teaching and play activities. Bring to the child's attention the skill components he or she has already achieved. Provide positive reinforcement and feedback for the child.

2. Use games that require expressive movement and that involve imitating, modeling, and demonstrating.

3. Observe and assess each child's maintenance at the end of two weeks. Repeat at the end of four weeks (if maintained) and six weeks after initial date of attainment.

▲ Box in the skill level to be maintained on the child's Class Record of Progress. Note the date the child attained target level of performance (defined by teacher alone or co-planned with parents).

▲ Two weeks after attainment, observe the child. Is the level maintained? If child does not demonstrate the skill components at the desired level of performance, indicate the skill components that need reteaching or reinforcing in the comments sheet on the Class Record of Progress. Reschedule teaching time, and co-plan with parents the home activities necessary to reinforce child's achievement of the skill components and maintenance of attainment.

▲ Continue to observe the child, and reteach and reinforce until the child maintains that level of performance for six weeks.

▲ Plan teaching activities incorporating these components so that the child can continually use and reinforce them and can acquire new ones over the year.

▲ When the child can understand it, make a check-list poster illustrating the child's achievements. Bring the child's attention to these skill components in various compatible play and game activities throughout the year. Have the child help others—a partner or a small group.

In Co-Planning with Parent(s)

1. Encourage the parent(s) to reinforce the child's achievement of the skill components in everyday play and living activities in the home.
▲ Provide key action words for the parent(s) to emphasize.
▲ Give the parent(s) a list of play and games to use in playing with the child, reinforcing the skill components the child has achieved and needs support to maintain.
▲ Give the parent(s) a list of expressive movement activities that can be done at home with the child, such as
   a. Expressing feelings (concepts) shown on TV or heard on the radio at home.
   b. Moving, imitating various animals in the home or neighborhood.
   c. Moving, imitating various moving objects.
2. Set up a time every two weeks to interact with the parent(s) and exchange feedback on the child's progress.

SINGING GAMES: SKILL LEVEL 1

Performance Objective

The child with ability to sing a song and clap or move hands, given a song known to the child, can demonstrate the following skill components three consecutive times:

Within a clear space of 20 feet, the child can

1. sing in unison with hand movements (clap or hand gestures) to beat of the music of two or more songs.

Action Words

(These words are found in the songs listed. They will differ depending on songs selected by teacher.)

Actions: Bake, blink, bumped, catch, clasp, close, come back, crawled, drink, fly away, jumping, knead, march, open, phoned, play, put, roll, run, shout, singing, sit, stood, throw, wash

Objects: Ball, bed, cake, clock, crocodile, cup, frog, hands, hill, house, man, monkeys, pointer, pinkie, pocket, pot, rabbit, ring, spider, spout, sun, tall man, thumbkin, water spout

Concepts: Away, back, down, happy, look, off, open, out, shut, tall, time, together, up, wide

Games

- Eensy Weensy Spider
- Five Green Speckled Frogs
- Five Little Chickadees
- Funny Clown
- If You're Happy
- Jack-in-the-Box
- Little Red Caboose
- My Hands
- My Little Puppy
- Open, Shut Them
- See My Fingers Walking
- Ten Little Jingle Bells
- This Old Man
- Where Is Thumbkin?

TEACHING ACTIVITIES

If a child requires assistance to respond,

1. give verbal cues and physical assistance.
Assist the child in moving hands to accompany music in the song. Place your hands over the child's hands initially, and then gradually have the child watch and imitate you singing and moving hands to the music. Give the child specific verbal instructions throughout. Sign language is a wonderful addition when teaching singing games.

2. give verbal cues with demonstration.
Use a model or have the child watch you move your hands to the song you sing together. Attach hand signs to the words to make the songs fun to sing.

If a child can respond without assistance,

3. give a verbal challenge in the form of a problem: "Who can do this?"
a. Move your hands and sing "Open, Shut Them."
b. Move your hands and sing "Five Little Chickadees."
c. Move your hands and sing "My Hands."
d. Move your hands and sing "Little Red Caboose."

4. introduce self-initiated learning activities.
Set up the equipment (record, tape recorder) and space for singing games. Provide time at the beginning of the lesson and free time for independent learning after the child understands the skills to be used. You may ask the child to create a game activity to play alone or with others (partner or small group), using the record or tapes.

5. Variations: Play a game, such as Eensy Weensy Spider or Open, Shut Them, that incorporates singing games.

SINGING GAMES: SKILL LEVEL 2

Performance Objective

The child with acquisition of Skill Level 1 and the ability to perform one or more locomotor skills, given a song known to the child, can demonstrate the following skill components three consecutive times:

Within a clear space of 20 feet, the child can

2. sing in unison with body movements (one or more locomotor skills) to beat of music of two or more songs.

Skills to Review

1. Sing in unison with hand movements (clap or hand gestures) to beat of music of two or more songs.

Action Words

(These words are found in the songs listed. They will differ depending on songs selected by teacher.)

Actions: Catch, falling, hit, hop, kick, lock, pour, ran, ringing, roll, run, sing, splashed, steam, stood, take, tip, touch, walked, wiggle

Objects: Ball, bell, bridges, handle, head, key, knees, policeman, pony, river, robin, shoulders, teapot, toes

Concepts: Circle, look, out, over, rip, short, stout, tall, this is the way, together, watch me

Games

- Bunny Hop
- Eensy Weensy Spider
- Head, Shoulders, Knees, Toes
- I'm a Little Teapot
- I Went to School One Morning
- Jack-in-the-Box
- Let's Walk Around the Circle
- London Bridge
- Open, Shut Them
- Ring Around the Rosy
- Wiggle Like a Snake

TEACHING ACTIVITIES

If a child requires assistance to respond,

1. give verbal cues and physical assistance.
Assist the child in moving body parts to accompany music in the song. Use your hands to physically assist the child, and then gradually have the child watch and imitate you singing and moving your body to the music. Give the child specific verbal instructions throughout. Sign language is a wonderful addition when teaching singing games.
2. give verbal cues with demonstration.
Use a model or have the child watch you move your body to the words in the song.

If a child can respond without assistance,

3. give a verbal challenge in the form of a problem: "Who can do this?"
a. Move your body to the words in "I'm a Little Teapot."
b. Move your body to the words in "Watch Me Move."
c. Move your body to the words in "Bunny Hop."
4. introduce self-initiated learning activities.
Set up the equipment (record, tape recorder) and space for singing games. Provide time at the beginning of the lesson and free time for independent learning after the child understands the skills to be used. You may ask the child to create a game activity to play alone or with others (partner or small group), using the record or tapes.
5. Variations: Play a game, such as Eensy Weensy Spider or Open, Shut Them, that incorporates singing games.

Performance Objective

The child with acquisition of Skill Level 2 or a level of performance appropriate for the child's level of functioning can maintain that level over six weeks.

Given activities that require the skill, the child can
1. play two or more games listed below at home or school, and
2. play with equipment selected by teacher and parent(s).

Skills to Review

1. Level 1 singing games. Sing in unison with hand movements (clap or hand gestures) to beat of music of two or more songs.
2. Level 2 singing games. Sing in unison with body movements (one or more locomotor skills) to beat of music of two or more songs.

Action Words

(These words are found in the songs listed. They will differ depending on songs selected by teacher.)

Actions: Bake, blink, bumped, catch, clasp, close, come back, crawled, drink, falling, fly away, hit, hop, jumping, kick, knead, lock, march, open, phoned, play, pour, put, roll, run, shout, sing, singing, sit, splashed, stood, take, throw, tip, touch, walked, wash, wiggle

Objects: Ball, bed, bell, cake, clock, crocodile, cup, frog, handle, hands, head, hill, house, key, knees, man, monkeys, pointer, pinkie, pocket, policeman, pony, pot, rabbit, ring, river, robin, shoulders, spider, spout, sun, tall man, teapot, thumbkin, toes, water spout

Concepts: Away, back, circle, down, happy, look, off, open, out, over, rip, short, shout, stout, tall, this is the way, time, together, up, watch me, wide

Games

- Bunny Hop
- Eensy Weensy Spider
- Five Green Speckled Frogs
- Five Little Chickadees
- Funny Clown
- Head, Shoulders, Knees, Toes
- If You're Happy
- I'm a Little Teapot
- I Went to School One Morning
- Jack-in-the-Box
- Let's Walk Around the Circle
- Little Red Caboose
- London Bridge
- Make a Fist
- My Hands
- My Little Puppy
- Open, Shut Them
- Ring Around the Rosy
- See My Fingers Walking
- Ten Little Jingle Bells
- This Old Man
- Where Is Thumbkin?
- Wiggle Like a Snake

TEACHING ACTIVITIES FOR MAINTENANCE

In Teaching

1. Provide the child with teaching cues (verbal and nonverbal, such as demonstration, modeling, imitating) for singing games that involve the skill components the child has achieved in compatible teaching and play activities. Bring to the child's attention the skill components he or she has already achieved. Provide positive reinforcement and feedback for the child.

2. Use games that require singing games and that involve imitating, modeling, and demonstrating.

3. Observe and assess each child's maintenance at the end of two weeks. Repeat at the end of four weeks (if maintained) and six weeks after initial date of attainment.

▲ Box in the skill level to be maintained on the child's Class Record of Progress. Note the date the child attained target level of performance (defined by teacher alone or co-planned with parents).

▲ Two weeks after attainment, observe the child. Is the level maintained? If child does not demonstrate the skill components at the desired level of performance, indicate the skill components that need reteaching or reinforcing in the comments sheet on the Class Record of Progress. Reschedule teaching time, and co-plan with parents the home activities necessary to reinforce child's achievement of the skill components and maintenance of attainment.

▲ Continue to observe the child, and reteach and reinforce until the child maintains that level of performance for six weeks.

▲ Plan teaching activities incorporating these components so that the child can continually use and reinforce them and can acquire new ones over the year.

▲ When the child can understand it, make a checklist poster illustrating the child's achievements. Bring the child's attention to these skill components in various compatible play and game activities throughout the year. Have the child help others—a partner or a small group.

In Co-Planning with Parent(s)

1. Encourage the parent(s) to reinforce the child's achievement of the skill components in everyday play and living activities in the home.

▲ Provide key action words for the parent(s) to emphasize.

▲ Give the parent(s) a list of play and games to use in playing with the child, thus reinforcing the skill components the child has achieved and needs support to maintain.

▲ Give the parent(s) a list of singing activities that can be done at home with the child, such as
   a. Moving your body or hands to the words in "Ring Around the Rosy."
   b. Moving body or hands to the words in "London Bridge."
   c. Moving body or hands to the words in "I Went to School One Morning."

2. Set up a time every two weeks to interact with the parent(s) and exchange feedback on the child's progress.

Checklists:
Individual and Class Records of Progress

A checklist is an objective score sheet for each rhythmic skill taught in the program. By observing and assessing each child's level of performance, you can identify the activities that will assist the child in reaching the performance objective. Use the same checklist to monitor the child's progress during instruction. When the child's performance level changes, you can upgrade the learning tasks (skill components) to the child's new skill level.

To Begin

Decide on one or more rhythmic activities to be taught in the program. Become familiar with the description of the performance objective for each activity selected. Review the scoring key on the checklist. Plan assessing activities for the selected skills. The number will depend on the class size, the needs of the children, and the help available to you. Set up testing stations similar to the learning stations. Some teachers use free-play time (after setting up equipment for the objective to be tested) to observe the children.

1. Begin assessing at Skill Level 2 for the particular objective. If the child cannot perform at Skill Level 2, assess for Skill Level 1. If the child demonstrates the skill components for Skill Level 2 (i.e., with modeling verbal cues, or no cues), the child has achieved functional competence. At the next skill level, Skill Level 3, the child demonstrates maintenance retention of the skill over time.

2. For some children with special needs, you may need to assess their levels of functioning before planning teaching activities. As in step 1, observe and assess the amount and type of assistance (cues) the child needs in descending order (i.e., from verbal cues to total manipulation).

Code	Amount and Type of Assistance
SI	Child initiates demonstrating the skill in the teaching and playing of activities
C	Child demonstrates the skill when given verbal cues with or without demonstration
A	Child demonstrates the skill when given partial assistance or total manipulation throughout the execution of the skill

Record, using the code above, the child's initial assistance level and progress in the comments column of the Class Record of Progress. For some children, this may be the most significant initial progress noted (i.e., from assistance to verbal cues and demonstration).

To Assess

1. Be sure all children are working on objectives at other stations while you are assessing at one station.

2. Make sure enough equipment is available for the skill to be tested.

3. For all rhythmic skills have two or three children at a testing station ready to be tested. (The other children in the class should be working at other learning stations.) Each child takes a turn on the command "go." At the end of the trials, record each child's performance on the score sheet.

4. You may need to modify the assessing activity for children's special needs by using inclines, providing a wider base and lower rise for steps, taking a child through the pattern or modeling the

activity, or using sign language or an interpreter. Other modifications are individual assessment or free play with the equipment. Use mats or movable walls to cut down on distractions.

To Adapt the Checklists

You can note children's skill components adaptations (i.e., physical devices or other changes) in the comments column on the Class Record of Progress. Other changes can be written under recommendations for individual children or the class. Modifications made for a child can be noted on the Individual Record of Progress. The Class Record of Progress can be adapted for an individual child. Record the name of the child rather than the class, and in the name column, record assessment dates. This adaptation may be needed for children whose progress is erratic, because it provides a base line assessment to find out where to begin teaching and evaluating the child's progress.

The Individual Record of Progress for the end-of-the-year report can be attached to the child's IEP (Individual Education Program) report. The record can also serve as a cumulative record for each child. Such records are very useful for new teachers, substitute teachers, aides, and volunteers, as well as parents. The format of the Individual Record of Progress can also be adapted for a Unit Report. The names of all the objectives for a unit—for example, walk-run endurance, running, catching a ball, and rolling a ball—are written rather than the names of the children. Book 8 illustrates the adaptation of the Individual Record of Progress for use in the Home Activities Program and for a Unit Report.

The checklists may be reproduced as needed to implement the play and motor skills program.

CLASS RECORD OF PROGRESS REPORT

CLASS _____ DATE _____

AGE/GRADE _____ TEACHER _____

SCHOOL _____

OBJECTIVE: MOVE TO AN EVEN BEAT

SCORING:	SKILL LEVEL 1		SKILL LEVEL 2		SKILL LEVEL 3	PRIMARY RESPONSES:
ASSESSMENT: _____ Date **X** = Achieved **O** = Not Achieved **/** = Partially Achieved REASSESSMENT: _____ Date ⊗ = Achieved Ø = Not Achieved	Three Consecutive Times					N = Not Attending NR = No Response UR = Unrelated Response O = Other (Specify in comments)
	Claps or moves (stamps, steps, taps, or moves trunk) to eight consecutive beats at moderate tempo.	Claps or moves (stamps, steps, taps, or moves trunk) to eight consecutive beats at fast tempo.	Moves (walks, runs, hops) to eight consecutive beats at moderate tempo.	Moves (walks, runs, hops) to eight consecutive beats at fast tempo.	Two or more play or game activities at home or school demonstrating skill components over six-week period.	
NAME	1	2	3	4	5	COMMENTS
1.						
2.						
3.						
4.						
5.						
6.						
7.						
8.						
9.						
10.						

Recommendations: Specific changes or conditions in planning for instructions, performance, or diagnostic testing procedures or standards. Please describe what worked best.

_____

_____

_____

_____

CLASS RECORD OF PROGRESS REPORT

CLASS _____ DATE _____

AGE/GRADE _____ TEACHER _____

SCHOOL _____

OBJECTIVE: MOVE TO AN UNEVEN BEAT

SCORING:	SKILL LEVEL 1		SKILL LEVEL 2	SKILL LEVEL 3	PRIMARY RESPONSES:
ASSESSMENT: _____Date **X** = Achieved **O** = Not Achieved **/** = Partially Achieved REASSESSMENT: _____Date **⊗** = Achieved **Ø** = Not Achieved	Three Consecutive Times				N = Not Attending NR = No Response UR = Unrelated Response O = Other (Specify in comments)
	Claps hands to two consecutive measures of uneven rhythm at moderate tempo.	Taps or stamps feet to two consecutive measures of uneven rhythm at moderate tempo.	Moves (gallops, skips, slides) to two consecutive measures of uneven rhythm at moderate tempo.	Two or more play or game activities at home or school demonstrating skill components over six-week period.	
NAME	1	2	3	4	COMMENTS
1.					
2.					
3.					
4.					
5.					
6.					
7.					
8.					
9.					
10.					

Recommendations: Specific changes or conditions in planning for instructions, performance, or diagnostic testing procedures or standards. Please describe what worked best.

_____

_____

_____

_____

_____

CLASS RECORD OF PROGRESS REPORT

CLASS _____   DATE _____

AGE/GRADE _____   TEACHER _____

SCHOOL _____

OBJECTIVE: ACCENT

SCORING:	SKILL LEVEL 1	SKILL LEVEL 2	SKILL LEVEL 3	PRIMARY RESPONSES:
ASSESSMENT: _____Date **X** = Achieved **O** = Not Achieved / = Partially Achieved REASSESSMENT: _____Date ⊗ = Achieved Ø = Not Achieved	Three Consecutive Times			N = Not Attending NR = No Response UR = Unrelated Response O = Other (Specify in comments)
	Claps or moves (stamps, steps, taps, or moves trunk), accenting the first beat of four consecutive measures.	Claps or moves (stamps, steps, taps), accenting the second, third, or fourth beat of four consecutive measures.	Two or more play or game activities at home or school demonstrating skill components over six-week period.	
NAME	1	2	3	COMMENTS
1.				
2.				
3.				
4.				
5.				
6.				
7.				
8.				
9.				
10.				

Recommendations: Specific changes or conditions in planning for instructions, performance, or diagnostic testing procedures or standards. Please describe what worked best.

_____

_____

_____

_____

_____

Class Record of Progress Report

CLASS _____   DATE _____

AGE/GRADE _____   TEACHER _____

SCHOOL _____

Objective: Expressive Movement

SCORING:	SKILL LEVEL 1			SKILL LEVEL 2		SKILL LEVEL 3	PRIMARY RESPONSES:
ASSESSMENT: _____Date **X** = Achieved **O** = Not Achieved **/** = Partially Achieved REASSESSMENT: _____Date **⊗** = Achieved **Ø** = Not Achieved	Three Consecutive Times						N = Not Attending NR = No Response UR = Unrelated Response O = Other (Specify in comments)
	Moves, imitating two out of three objects.	Moves, imitating two out of three gestures.	Moves, expressing two out of three feelings.	Performs series of movements, communicating to others two out of three daily events or activities.	Performs series of movements, communicating to others two out of three play events or activities.	Two or more play or game activities at home or school demonstrating skill components over six-week period.	
NAME	1	2	3	4	5	6	COMMENTS
1.							
2.							
3.							
4.							
5.							
6.							
7.							
8.							
9.							
10.							

Recommendations: Specific changes or conditions in planning for instructions, performance, or diagnostic testing procedures or standards. Please describe what worked best.

_____

_____

_____

_____

_____

_____

CLASS RECORD OF PROGRESS REPORT

CLASS _____   DATE _____

AGE/GRADE _____   TEACHER _____

SCHOOL _____

OBJECTIVE: SINGING GAMES

SCORING:	SKILL LEVEL 1	SKILL LEVEL 2	SKILL LEVEL 3	PRIMARY RESPONSES:
ASSESSMENT: _____Date **X** = Achieved **O** = Not Achieved / = Partially Achieved REASSESSMENT: _____Date ⊗ = Achieved Ø = Not Achieved	Three Consecutive Times			N = Not Attending NR = No Response UR = Unrelated Response O = Other (Specify in comments)
	Sings in unison with hand movements (clap or hand gestures) to beat of music of two or more songs.	Sings in unison with body movements (one or more locomotor skills) to beat of music of two or more songs.	Two or more play or game activities at home or school demonstrating skill components over six-week period.	
NAME	1	2	3	COMMENTS
1.				
2.				
3.				
4.				
5.				
6.				
7.				
8.				
9.				
10.				

Recommendations: Specific changes or conditions in planning for instructions, performance, or diagnostic testing procedures or standards. Please describe what worked best.

_____

_____

_____

_____

_____

INDIVIDUAL RECORD OF PROGRESS

Area: Rhythmic Skills

CHILD: _____

LEVEL: _____

YEAR: _____

TEACHER: _____

SCHOOL: _____

Marking Period	*Date*
Fall Conference (white)	from ____ to ____
Winter Conference (yellow)	from ____ to ____
Spring Conference (pink)	from ____ to ____
End-of-Year (cumulative) Report (blue)	from ____ to ____

Preprimary Play and Motor Skills Activity Program

The Individual Record of Progress lists all of the objectives in which your child receives instruction during the play and motor skills program. The information reported on your child's Individual Record of Progress shows your child's entry performance and progress for a marking period. The end-of-the-year report represents your child's Individual Education Program (IEP) for the objectives selected and taught during the year.

Each objective is broken into small, measurable steps or skill components. This assists the teacher to assess what your child already knew before teaching began and to determine which step to start teaching first. One of the following symbols is marked by each step or skill component of the objective:

X = The child already knew how to perform this step before teaching it began.

O = The child did not know how to perform this step before teaching it began or after instruction of it ended.

⊗ = The child did not know how to perform this step before teaching it began, but did learn how to do it during the instruction period.

This information should be helpful to you in planning home activities to strengthen your child's play and motor skills.

Comments

_____

_____

_____

_____

_____

_____

_____

_____

MOVE TO AN EVEN BEAT

Date: _____

Within a space of 20 feet
Three consecutive times

____ Claps or moves (stamps, steps, taps, or moves trunk) to eight consecutive beats at moderate tempo.

____ Claps or moves (stamps, steps, taps, or moves trunk) to eight consecutive beats at fast tempo.

____ Moves (walks, runs, hops) to eight consecutive beats at moderate tempo.

____ Moves (walks, runs, hops) to eight consecutive beats at fast tempo.

____ Demonstrates above skill in two or more play or game activities at home or school over a six-week period.

MOVE TO AN UNEVEN BEAT

Date: _____

Within a space of 20 feet
Three consecutive times

____ Claps hands to two consecutive measures of uneven rhythm at moderate tempo.

____ Taps or stamps feet to two consecutive measures of uneven rhythm at moderate tempo.

____ Moves (gallops, skips, slides) to two consecutive measures of uneven rhythm at moderate tempo.

____ Demonstrates above skill in two or more play or game activities at home or school over a six-week period.

ACCENT

Date: _____

Within a space of 20 feet
Three consecutive times

____ Claps or moves (stamps, steps, taps, or moves trunk), accenting the first beat of four consecutive measures.

____ Claps or moves (stamps, steps, taps, or moves trunk), accenting the second, third, or fourth beat of four consecutive measures.

____ Demonstrates above skill in two or more play or game activities at home or school over a six-week period.

EXPRESSIVE MOVEMENT

Date: _____

Within a clear space of 20 feet
Three consecutive times

____ Moves, imitating two out of three objects.

____ Moves, imitating two out of three gestures.

____ Performs series of movements, communicating to others two out of three daily events or activities.

____ Performs series of movements, communicating to others two out of three play events or activities.

____ Demonstrates above skill in two or more play or game activities at home or school over a six-week period.

SINGING GAMES

Date: _____

Within a clear space of 20 feet
Three consecutive times

____ Sings in unison with hand movements (clap or hand gestures) to beat of music of two or more songs.

____ Sings in unison with body movements (one or more locomotor skills) to beat of music of two or more songs.

____ Demonstrates above skill in two or more play or game activities at home or school over a six-week period.

Games

Game Selection

The following game sheets will help you select and plan game activities. They include the names of the games in alphabetical order, formation, directions, equipment, rhythmic skills, and type of play activity. Consider the following points when selecting games:

1. Skills and objectives of your program

2. Interest of the child

3. Equipment and rules

4. Adaptability of physical difficulty level in order to match each child's ability

5. Activity for healthy growth and development

6. Social play skill development, such as taking turns, sharing equipment, playing with others, and following and leading

Games can foster creativity. Children enjoy making up, interpreting, and creating their own activities, whether playing alone, with a partner, or with a small group. The time you take to provide opportunities for each child to explore and create will be well spent. One further note. Children can easily create or adapt games matched to their mobility, even if limited by crutches, braces, or wheelchairs. Rhythmic activities involve moving from here to there. These children easily comprehend how to get to "there" with their own expertise for movement.

Following are some suggestions for adapting the physical difficulty level of games and a sequential list of social play development.

Adapting Games

To Change	*Use*	*Example*
1. Boundaries	Larger or smaller space	In Five Little Chickadees, enlarge circle by two giant steps.
2. Equipment	Larger or smaller sizes, weights, or heights, or specially adapted equipment for some children (such as guide-rails, inclines rather than stairs, brightly colored mats)	Use drums or other instruments of different sizes in Follow the Drum.
3. Rules	More or fewer rules	In Hit the Drum, stamp your feet to the even beat, then to the uneven beat.

4. Actions	More or fewer actions to be performed at one time; play in stationary positions, using various body parts	To Count to Six Fast, clap hands and stomp feet.
5. Time of play	Longer or shorter time; frequent rest periods	In Even-Uneven Tempo Relay, move to beat for one minute, then for two minutes.

To adapt games to other special needs, you might also use buddies and spotters, sign language gestures, or place the child near leader.

Sequential Development of Social Play

Sequence	*Description*	*Example of Play Activity*
Individual Play	Child plays alone and independently with toys that are different from those used by other children within speaking distance.	Child plays Jack-in-the-Box on classroom rug, while other children sing "Ten Little Jingle Bells" or "My Little Puppy," while sitting on rug.
Parallel Play	Child plays independently beside, rather than with, other children.	Child plays Wiggle Like a Snake, while other children also play the game. No interaction between children.
Associate Play	Child plays with other children. There is interaction between children, but there are no common goals.	Child plays Ten Little Indians in a group but functions independently.
Cooperative Play	Child plays within a group organized for playing formal games. Group is goal directed.	Children play Farmer in the Dell and London Bridge together.

GAME SHEET LESSON PLANS

GAMES	ORGANIZATION		DESCRIPTION/INSTRUCTIONS	EQUIPMENT	SKILLS	TYPE OF PLAY ACTIVITY
Around We Go	Circle	(circle formation diagram with T)	Children form circle with hands joined. Say, "Around we go, around we go, one big circle marching so. Down we go, down we go, one big circle sinking so." Slowly go down. "Up we go, up we go, one big circle rising so." All rise slowly. "In we go, in we go, one big circle slowly so." Move toward center. "Out we go, out we go, one big circle stretching so." Walk backward to place and stretch."	Drum and stick	Even tempo (4/4), accent	Small group, large group
A Tiny Little Mouse	Scatter	(scatter formation diagram)	Children sing song and move to it. "There's such a tiny little mouse, living safely in my house. Out at night he'll softly creep, when everyone is fast asleep. But always in the light of day, he'll softly, softly creep away."	None	Singing games and expressive movement	Individual, partners, small group, large group
Baa Baa Black Sheep	Circle	(circle formation diagram)	Organize children into circle. They sing the song and clap hands or move to beat of drum. "Baa, baa, black sheep, have you any wool?" Pretend to be sheep with horns. "Yes sir, yes sir, three bags full." Nod head twice, hold up three fingers. "One for my master, one for my dame," (hold up finger to emphasize one, and repeat action) "and one for the little boy who lives in the lane." Again hold up one finger.	Drum, stick, record	Move to even beat (4/4), singing games, expressive movement	Individual, partners, small group, large group

Game Sheet Lesson Plans

Games	Organization	Description/Instructions	Equipment	Skills	Type of Play Activity
Brother John	Scatter X X X X X X X X X	Children sing song and clap or move to beat of music. "Are you sleeping, are you sleeping? Brother John, Brother John. Morning bells are ringing, morning bells are ringing. Ding, ding, dong; ding, ding, dong." 1. Children walk around asking the question of each other. 2. Continue to walk and talk to each other. 3. Hold their heads and sway back and forth. 4. Pretend to ring bells.	None	Even beat, singing games, expressive movement	Individual, partners, small group, large group
Bunny Hop	Scatter X X X X X X X X X	Children sing song and move or clap hands to beat. "I can hop like a bunny hops, hopping up and down. Hopping, hopping all day long. Hopping all around."	Drum, sticks, records	Singing games, expressive movement	Individual, partners, small group, large group

Game Sheet Lesson Plans

Games	Organization	Description/Instructions	Equipment	Skills	Type of Play Activity
Catch a Falling Star	Scatter X X X X X X X X	Children sing song and move or clap hands to beat. "Catch a falling star, put it in your pocket, save it for a rainy day. Catch a falling star, put it in your pocket, never let it fade away."	Drum, sticks, records	Singing games, expressive movement	Individual, partners, small group, large group
Count to Six Fast	Circle X X T X X X X X X	Tell children to listen to fast drumbeats. Say, "1, 2, 3, 4, 5, 6, ready, go." Clap hands for 8 beats along with verbal cues. Demonstrate moving hips or other body parts fast on 8 beats. Say, "1, 2, 3, 4, 5, 6, ready, go."	Drum, stick	Move to even beat (4/4)	Individual, partners, small group, large group

GAME SHEET LESSON PLANS

GAMES	ORGANIZATION	DESCRIPTION/INSTRUCTIONS	EQUIPMENT	SKILLS	TYPE OF PLAY ACTIVITY
Crocodile Song	Scatter	Children sing song and move or clap hands to beat. "Oh, she sailed away on a bright and sunny day on the back of a crocodile." Hands flat on top of one another. "'You see,' said she, 'He's as tame as he can be.'" Stroke the back of one hand with other. "'I'll ride him down the Nile.'" Hands on top of one another, "swim" them. "Well, the croc winked his eye" (wink eye) "as he waved his friends good-bye," (wave) "wearing a happy smile." Show smile. "At the end of the ride the lady was inside," (point to tummy) "and the smile was on the crocodile." Smile. "He ate her all up! The smile was on the crocodile! Yeah!"	Drum, sticks, records	Singing games, expressive movement	Individual, partners, small group, large group
Diddle Diddle Dumpling	Scatter	Children sing song and clap or move to beat of music. "Diddle, diddle dumpling, my son John" (do a jig in place, turning around) "went to bed with his stockings on." Pretend to sleep, with hands alongside face, and then point to stockings. "One shoe off and one shoe on." Bounce on one foot, thrusting other foot forward; reverse feet. "Diddle, diddle dumpling, my son John." Again, do jig in place, turning around.	None	Singing games, expressive movement	Individual, partners, small group, large group

Game Sheet Lesson Plans

Games	Organization	Description/Instructions	Equipment	Skills	Type of Play Activity
Eensy Weensy Spider	Scatter	Children sing song and move or clap hands to beat. "Eensy weensy spider, crawled up the water spout. Down came the rain and washed the spider out. Out came the sun, and dried up all the rain. So the eensy weensy spider crawled up the spout again."	Drum, sticks, record	Singing games, expressive movement	Individual, partners, small group, large group
Even-Uneven Tempo Relay	Lines	Have children line up in three teams. On the beat of the drum, move quickly to the wall and back again. First team to move through all players is the winner.	Drum, stick	Even and uneven beat	Relay; individual, partners, small group, large group

GAME SHEET LESSON PLANS

GAMES	ORGANIZATION	DESCRIPTION/INSTRUCTIONS	EQUIPMENT	SKILLS	TYPE OF PLAY ACTIVITY

The Farmer in the Dell	Circle
	
	x x x
	x x
	x x x
		Children listen to the beat of drum as they sing the song and clap hands or move to beat of song.
		"The farmer in the dell,
		The farmer in the dell,
		Hi-yo the dairy-o,
		The farmer in the dell."
		  One child stands in center and is the farmer.
		"The farmer takes a wife,
		The farmer takes a wife.
		Hi-yo the dairy-o,
		The farmer takes a wife."
		  Child chooses another to be wife and they hold hands.
		"The wife takes the nurse,
		The wife takes the nurse.
		Hi-yo the dairy-o,
		The wife takes the nurse."
		  Each new person takes another until they reach the cheese.
		"The nurse takes the child (etc.).
		The child takes the dog (etc.).
		The dog takes the cat (etc.). The cat takes the mouse (etc.). The mouse takes the cheese (etc.).
		The cheese stands alone."
		  Then all children go back into circle and move around the cheese.
			Drum, stick, record	Move to even beat (4/4), singing games, expressive movement	Small group, large group

Game Sheet Lesson Plans

Games	Organization	Description/Instructions	Equipment	Skills	Type of Play Activity
Five Green Speckled Frogs	Scatter	Children sing song and move or clap hands to beat. "Five green speckled frogs" (show five fingers) "sat on a speckled log," (squat like a frog) "eating the most delicious bugs—yum-yum." Rub tummy. "One jumped into the pool," (make jumping movement) "where it was nice and cool." Fan self with fan. "Now there are four green speckled frogs—glub, glub." Show four fingers, continue until there are none.	Drum, sticks, record	Singing games, expressive movement	Individual, partners, small group, large group
Five Little Chickadees	Circle	All children form large circle, except for five children in center. Sing song. On words "One flew away," first chickadee jumps up and joins large circle. Repeat until all fly home. "Five little chicka-dees, sitting near the door, one flew away, and then there were four. Four little chickadees, sitting in a tree, one flew away, then there were three. Three little chickadees, looking at you, one flew away, and then there were two. Two little chickadees, sitting in the sun, one flew away, and then there was one. One little chickadee, left all alone, it flew away, and then there were none. Chickadee, chickadee, happy and gay, chickadee, chickadee, fly, fly away."	None	Singing games, expressive movement	Small group, large group

Game Sheet Lesson Plans

Games	Organization	Description/Instructions	Equipment	Skills	Type of Play Activity
Five Little Monkeys	Scatter X X X X X X X X	Children sing song and move or clap hands to beat. "Five little monkeys jumping on the bed." Jump up and down. "One fell off and bumped his head." Hold head. "Mother phoned the doctor." Dial phone. "The doctor said, 'no more jumping on the bed!'" Scowl and shake finger; continue until there are no monkeys.	Drum, sticks, records	Singing games, expressive movement	Individual, partners, small group, large group
Follow the Drum	Scatter X X X X X X X X	While sitting, have children clap to the rhythm of the drumbeat. Say, "Now stand up and make your feet go like the drumbeat." 4/4: walk, walk, walk, walk; step, step, step, step. "Listen carefully to the drumbeat; make your feet walk (hop, run) to the beat." Children should stand still when drumbeat stops.	Drum	Move to even and uneven beat, accent	Individual, partners, small group, large group

Game Sheet Lesson Plans

Games	Organization	Description/Instructions	Equipment	Skills	Type of Play Activity
Funny Clown	Circle or scatter (diagram of X marks in circle)	Children sing the song and move as they sing. "I am a funny clown. I move like a funny clown. I jump, I skip and run. I stop and have a lot of fun."	None	Singing games, expressive movement	Individual, partners, small group, large group
Happy Story	Scatter (diagram of scattered X marks)	Have children sitting scattered but where they can see teacher. Say, "Listen to a happy story. Johnny woke all excited because he was going to go to a park to play. He *jumped* and *smiled* and *turned* all around. Then he *skipped* and *ran*. He was very happy! What did he do to show how happy he was? Do this. Move like you are *happy*." Follow with stories for other feelings.	Picture of feelings: happy, sad, angry, fearful	Expressive movements	Individual, partners, small group, large group

Game Sheet Lesson Plans

Games	Organization	Description/Instructions	Equipment	Skills	Type of Play Activity
Head, Shoulders, Knees, and Toes	Scatter X X X X X X X X	Children sing song and move or tap body parts to beat. "Head, shoulders, knees, and toes, knees, and toes. Head, shoulders, knees, and toes, knees, and toes, knees, and toes."	Drum, sticks, records	Singing games, expressive movement	Individual, partners, small group, large group
Here's a Cup	Scatter X X X X X X X X	Children sing song and move or clap hands to beat. "Here's a cup and here's a cup." Make a circle with thumb and index finger of open hand, extend arm and repeat. "And here's a pot." Make fist with other hand and extend thumb for spout. "Pour a cup, and pour a cup," (tip fist to pour) "and have a drink with me." Make drinking motions.	Drum, sticks, records	Singing games, expressive movement	Individual, partners, small group, large group

Game Sheet Lesson Plans

Games	Organization	Description/Instructions	Equipment	Skills	Type of Play Activity
Hit the Beat	Circle X T X X X X X X X	Children listen to accented beat. Say, "Hit the beat on count one. *One*, two, three, go. *One*, two, three, four." Repeat 3 more times. "Hit the beat on count *two*. One, *two*, three, go! One, *two*, three four." Repeat 3 more times. "Hit the beat on *three*. One, two, *three*, go! One, two, *three*, four." Repeat 3 more times. "Let's go around the circle. I'll beat the drum, and you clap to the loud beat."	Drum, sticks	Even tempo, accent	Individual, small group, large group
If You're Happy	Scatter X X X X X X	Children sing song and move or clap hands to beat. "If you're happy and you know it, clap your hands. If you're happy and you know it, clap your hands. If you're happy and you know it, and you really want to show it, if you're happy and you know it, clap your hands. "If you're angry and you know it, stamp your feet (etc.)." "If you're sad and you know it, you can cry (etc.)."	Drum, sticks, record	Singing games, expressive movement	Individual, partner, small group, large group

Game Sheet Lesson Plans

Games	Organization	Description/Instructions	Equipment	Skills	Type of Play Activity
I'm a Little Teapot	Scatter	Children sing song and move or clap hands to beat. "I'm a little teapot, short and stout. Here is my handle, here is my spout. When I get all steamed up, hear me shout, 'Tip me over and pour me out.'"	Piano (music)	Expressive communication	Individual, partners, small group, large group
Isn't It Fun?	Scatter	Say, "Let's learn a song and you do what I do." "Oh, isn't it it fun to wave hello, wave hello, wave hello? Oh, isn't it it fun to wave hello? I like to wave hello." "Let's sing together and wave when we say *wave hello*. I'll point to one of you at a time and then you wave to me." Can also wave goodbye, nod head yes, shake head no, move like various animals.	Piano (music)	Expressive communication	Individual, partners, small group, large group

GAME SHEET LESSON PLANS

GAMES	ORGANIZATION	DESCRIPTION/INSTRUCTIONS	EQUIPMENT	SKILLS	TYPE OF PLAY ACTIVITY
I Went to School One Morning	Scatter	Children sing song and move or clap hands to beat. "I went to school one morning and I walked like this, walked like this, walked like this. I went to school one morning and I walked like this on my way to school. "I saw a little robin and he hopped like this (etc.). "I saw a shiny river and I splashed like this (etc.). "I saw a little pony and he galloped like this (etc.). "I saw a tall policeman and he stood like this (etc.). "I heard the school bell ringing and I ran like this (etc.)."	Drum, sticks, records	Singing games, expressive movement	Individual, partners, small group, large group
Jack-in-the-Box	Scatter	Children sing song and move or clap hands to beat. "Jack-in-the-box is out of sight" (children crouch down) "when the cover's fastened tight." Clap on word *tight.* "Press the lid and up he goes." Jump up. "Jack-in-the-box with the long red nose." Point to nose.	Drum, sticks, records	Singing games, expressive movement	Individual, partners, small group, large group

GAME SHEET LESSON PLANS

GAMES	ORGANIZATION	DESCRIPTION/INSTRUCTIONS	EQUIPMENT	SKILLS	TYPE OF PLAY ACTIVITY
Let's Walk Around the Circle	Scatter	Children sing song and move or clap hands to beat. (1) "Let's walk around the circle, let's walk around the circle, let's walk around the circle as we have done before." (2) "Let's run around the circle." (3) "Let's skip." (4) "Let's hop." (5) "Let's jump." (6) "Let's walk fast." (7) "Let's walk slow." (8) "Let's stand in the middle of the circle."	Drum, sticks, records	Singing games, expressive movement	Individual, partners, small group, large group
Little Rabbit	Scatter	Children sing song and move or clap hands to beat. "In a cabin in the woods a little old man by the window stood. Saw a rabbit hopping by knocking at his door. 'Help me, help me, sir,' he said, 'before the farmer shoots me dead.' 'Come little rabbit, come with me, happy we will always be.'"	Drum, sticks, records	Singing games, expressive movement	Individual, partners, small group, large group

GAME SHEET LESSON PLANS

GAMES	ORGANIZATION	DESCRIPTION/INSTRUCTIONS	EQUIPMENT	SKILLS	TYPE OF PLAY ACTIVITY
Little Red Caboose	Line X X X X X X X X X X	Children line up in two lines, put hands on the child's shoulders in front of each of them. Sing and move to song. "Little red caboose, little red caboose, little red caboose behind the train. Smokestack on its back, rumblin' down the track, little red caboose behind the train. Toot! "Little red caboose, little red caboose, little red caboose behind the train. Coming round the bend, hanging on the end, little red caboose behind the train. Toot!"	None	Singing games, expressive movement	Individual, partners

Game Sheet Lesson Plans

Games	Organization	Description/Instructions	Equipment	Skills	Type of Play Activity
London Bridge	Lines X X X↑ X X X X X	Two children holding hands high are the bridge. Others walk under bridge singing song. Clap to verses. (1) "London Bridge is falling down, falling down, falling down. London Bridge is falling down, my fair lady" (2) "Build it up with iron bars" (etc.). (3) "Iron bars will rust away" (etc.). (4) "Build it up with gold and silver" (etc.). (5) "Gold and silver I have not" (etc.). (6) "Build it up with pins and needles" (etc.). (7) "Pins and needles rust and bend" (etc.). (8) "Build it up with penny loaves" (etc.). (9) "Penny loaves will tumble down" (etc.). (10) "Here's a prisoner I have got" (etc.). (11) "What's the prisoner done to you?" (etc.). (12) "Stole my watch and bracelet too" (etc.). (13) "What'll you take to set him (her) free?" (etc.). (14) "One hundred pounds will set him (her) free" (etc.). (15) "One hundred pounds we do not have" (etc.). (16) "Then off to prison he (she) must go" (etc.). All children pass under bridge in a single line. When the words "My fair lady" are sung, the bridge falls and the child caught is a prisoner. He or she must choose either gold or silver and must stand behind the side of the bridge representing that choice. When all have been caught, the game ends with a tug-of-war.	None	Move to uneven beat, singing games, expressive movement	Small group, large group

GAME SHEET LESSON PLANS

GAMES	ORGANIZATION	DESCRIPTION/INSTRUCTIONS	EQUIPMENT	SKILLS	TYPE OF PLAY ACTIVITY
Mary Had a Little Lamb	Scatter ✗ ✗ ✗ ✗ ✗ ✗ ✗	Children sing song and clap or move to beat of music. "Mary had a little lamb, little lamb, little lamb. Mary had a little lamb; its fleece was white as snow." Mary pets her lamb and pretends to like it very much. Lamb crouches down. "And ev'rywhere that Mary went, Mary went, Mary went, ev'rywhere that Mary went, the lamb was sure to go." Lamb follows Mary around wherever she goes. "It followed her to school one day, school one day, school one day. It followed her to school one day, which teacher did not like." Mary brings her lamb to school, and teacher shakes head.	None	Singing games, expressive movement	Individual, partners, small group, large group

Game Sheet Lesson Plans

Games	Organization	Description/Instructions	Equipment	Skills	Type of Play Activity
Monkey See, Monkey Do	Scatter	Children sing song and move or clap hands to beat. "When I touch, touch, touch my eyes, the monkey touch, touch, touch his eyes. Monkey see and monkey do. The monkey does the same as you. "When I blink, blink, blink my eyes (etc.). " . . . close, close, close . . . " . . . open, open, open . . . " . . . look up and look down . . . "	Drum, sticks, records	Singing games, expressive movement	Individual, partners, small group, large group
Mulberry Bush	Circle	Children sit for clapping or stand for moving. Say, "Clap your hands with me and sing" (4/4 rhythm). "This is the way we clap our hands, clap our hands, clap our hands. This is the way we clap our hands, early in the morning. "This is the way we move our hips, move our hips, move our hips. This is the way we move our hips, early in the morning." Continue with other movements.	Drum and stick; piano and music	Move to even beat, singing games	Individual, partners, small group, large group

GAME SHEET LESSON PLANS

GAMES	ORGANIZATION	DESCRIPTION/INSTRUCTIONS	EQUIPMENT	SKILLS	TYPE OF PLAY ACTIVITY
My Airplane	Scatter	Children sing song and move to it. "My airplane has great big wings. And a propeller that goes up, up, up and down, down, down."	None	Singing games, expressive movement	Individual, partners, small group, large group
My Hands	Circle	Children move hands as they sing song. "I raise my hands up high. Now on the floor they lie. Now high, now low. Now reach up to the sky. "I spread my hands out wide. Now behind my back they hide. Now wide; now hide. Now I put them at my side. "I give my head a shake, shake, shake. Now not a move I make. Now shake, shake, shake. Not a move I make. Now my whole self I shake."	None	Singing games, expressive movement	Individual, partners, small group, large group

GAME SHEET LESSON PLANS

GAMES	ORGANIZATION	DESCRIPTION/INSTRUCTIONS	EQUIPMENT	SKILLS	TYPE OF PLAY ACTIVITY
My Little Puppy	Circle or scatter × × × × × × × ×	Children move in a circle as they sing song and express each action of puppy. "My little puppy's name is Rags. He eats so much that his tummy sags. His ears flip-flop, his tail wig-wags. And when he walks, he zigs and zags."	None	Singing games, expressive movement	Individual, partners, small group, large group
One, Two, Buckle My Shoe	Circle × × × T × × × × ×	Have children listen to beat (4/4). "One, two, buckle my shoe. Three, four, close the door." Say, "Clap, clap, clap your hands." Can also move body parts or stomp feet.	Drum, stick	Move to uneven beat	Individual, partners, small group, large group

Game Sheet Lesson Plans

Games	Organization	Description/Instructions	Equipment	Skills	Type of Play Activity
Open, Shut Them	Scatter X X X X X X X	Children sing song and move or clap hands to beat. "Open, shut them. Open, shut them. Give your hands a clap. Open, shut them. Open, shut them. Put them in your lap."	Drum, sticks, records	Singing games, expressive movement	Individual, partners, small group, large group
Pat-a-Cake	Scatter X X X X X X X	Children sing song and move or clap hands to beat. "Pat-a-cake, pat-a-cake, baker-man, bake me a cake as fast as you can. Roll it and knead it and mark it with a 'B' (or other letter) and there'll be cake for you and me."	Drum, sticks	Singing games, expressive movement	Individual, partners, small group, large group

GAME SHEET LESSON PLANS

GAMES	ORGANIZATION	DESCRIPTION/INSTRUCTIONS	EQUIPMENT	SKILLS	TYPE OF PLAY ACTIVITY
Ring Around the Rosy	Scatter (X's scattered)	Children sing song and move or clap hands to beat. "Ring around the rosy, a pocket full of posies. Ashes, ashes, we all fall down."	Drum, sticks, records	Singing games, expressive movement	Individual, partners, small group, large group
See My Fingers Walking	Scatter (X's scattered)	Children sing song and move or clap to beat. "See my fingers walking, walking, all together in a row. See my fingers walking, walking, all together to and fro. There is a big house, tall and wide. Knock at the door and walk inside!"	Drum, sticks, records	Singing games, expressive movement	Individual, partners, small group, large group

Game Sheet Lesson Plans

Games	Organization	Description/Instructions	Equipment	Skills	Type of Play Activity
Ten Little Indians	Circle × × × × × × × ×	Ten children, numberd 1–10, are in center of circle. "One little, two little, three little Indians; four little, five little, six little Indians; seven little, eight little, nine little Indians; ten little Indian braves (squaws)." During the second repetition of the music, the Indians in the center do an Indian dance, each in his or her own way. Sing the verse again, but this time, the Indians in the center return to the circle when their numbers are sung. During the last repetition, all children dance as Indians, moving in any direction they wish, not retaining the circle formation. Repeat dance with another set of Indians.	Drum, sticks	Even beat, singing games, expressive movement	Small group

Game Sheet Lesson Plans

Games	Organization	Description/Instructions	Equipment	Skills	Type of Play Activity

Ten Little Jingle Bells	Lines
	
	L
	X X X X X X X X X
	X X X X X X X X X
		Children line up in rows of ten behind leader (horse) and sing song and do what song says.
		    "Ten little jingle bells hung in a row, ten little jingle bells helped the horse go. Merrily, merrily over the snow, merrily, merrily sleighing we go.
		    "One little jingle bell fell in the snow, nine little jingle bells helped the horse go. Merrily, merrily over the snow, merrily, merrily sleighing we go."
			None	Singing games, expressive movement	Individual, partners, small group, large group

This Old Man	Scatter
	
	    X
	  X X
	X X
	    X X
	  X X
		Children sing song and move or clap hands to beat.
		    "This old man, he played one, he played nick-nack on my thumb, with a nick-nack patty-wack, give a dog a bone, this old man came rolling home.
		    "This old man, he played two, he played nick-nack on my shoe. . .
		    "Three-knee . . . four-door . . . five-hive . . . six-sticks . . . seven-up in heaven . . . eight-plate . . . nine-vine . . . ten-once again."
			Drum, sticks, records	Singing games, expressive movement	Individual, partners, small group, large group

Game Sheet Lesson Plans

Games	Organization	Description/Instructions	Equipment	Skills	Type of Play Activity
Twinkle, Twinkle Little Star	Scatter X X X X X X X X X	Have children listen to beat, then clap hands or move to music. "Twinkle, twinkle, little star. How I wonder what you are. Up above the world so high, like a diamond in the sky. Twinkle, twinkle, little star. How I wonder what you are." Children have arms extended overhead, with fingers extended and moving. Each child takes seven tiptoe steps toward the center of the circle. Continue with seven tiptoe steps in place, making a full turn. Each child makes a circle with arms and hands, rocking back and forth.	None	Move to even beat, singing games	Individual, partners, small group, large group

GAME SHEET LESSON PLANS

GAMES	ORGANIZATION	DESCRIPTION/INSTRUCTIONS	EQUIPMENT	SKILLS	TYPE OF PLAY ACTIVITY
Two Little Blackbirds	Scatter ⨯ ⨯ ⨯ ⨯ ⨯ ⨯	Children sing song and move or clap hands to beat. "Two little blackbirds" (close fists, extend index finger) "sitting on a hill. One named Jack" (talk to one index finger) "and the other named Jill." Talk to other index finger. "Fly away, Jack," ("toss" one index finger over shoulder) "fly away, Jill." "Toss" other index finger over shoulder. "Come, back Jack," (hands separately with index fingers extended) "come back, Jill."	Drum, sticks, records	Singing games, expressive movement	Individual, partners, small group, large group

Game Sheet Lesson Plans

Games	Organization	Description/Instructions	Equipment	Skills	Type of Play Activity
Where Is Thumbkin?	Scatter X X X X X X X X	Children sing song and move or clap hands to beat. "Where is Thumbkin? Where is Thumbkin?" Put hands behind back. "Here I am." Show other thumb. "How are you this morning?" Bend one thumb. "Very well, thank you." Bend other thumb. "Run and play, run and play." Put thumbs behind back. Repeat above, "talking" with successive fingers: (2) Where is pointer? (3) Where is tall man? (4) Where is ring man? (5) Where is pinkie?	Drum, sticks, record	Singing games, expressive movement	Individual, partners, small group, large group
Wiggle Like a Snake	Scatter X X X X X X X	Children sing song and move to it. Encourage them to act out song. "Wiggle like a snake, hop like a bunny, climb like a monkey, now do something funny."	None	Singing games, expressive movement	Individual, partners, small group, large group

GAME SHEET LESSON PLANS

GAMES	ORGANIZATION	DESCRIPTION/INSTRUCTIONS	EQUIPMENT	SKILLS	TYPE OF PLAY ACTIVITY
Yankee Doodle	Partners or circle x—x x + + x—x + + + x—x + + +	One child is pony; one child is Yankee Doodle. Sing song. Clap or move to music. "Yankee Doodle went to town, a-riding on a pony. Stuck a feather in his cap and called it macaroni. Yankee Doodle doodle doo, Yankee Doodle dandy. All the lassies are so smart and sweet as sugar candy."	None	Move to even beat, singing games, expressive movement	Individual, partners, small group, large group
Zoo Song	Scatter X X X X X X X X	Children sing song and move to it. Encourage each child to select an animal, and everybody imitate that animal. "See the animals in the zoo, in the zoo, in the zoo. See the animals in the zoo, and you can do it too."	None	Singing games, expressive movement	Individual, partners, small group, large group